THE CHANGING CONDITIONS OF POLITICS

J. A. Corry, one of Canada's outstanding political scientists, in the Alan B. Plaunt Lectures for 1963 has contributed a brilliant and provocative analysis of the changed world in which politics and students of politics must operate today, He suggests first that political studies can no longer be confined to the frame long held. adequate. The eighteenth-century view of man as essentially rational suited an age of individualism and liberal optimism but is inadequate for politics in our mass society: here theology has something to contribute. Political science has in the past confined its attention to the operation of governments and political parties but has not for this age taken enough account of the influence of the social structure as a whole on political behaviour: here is where sociology may speak. With this background Principal Corry talks of the difficulties of understanding our present-day political world with the stock of political ideas and theories hitherto usually relied on for the purpose. He goes on to look at some aspects of the collectivist, mass society we live in today and to consider how far these may be producing new dimensions in political behaviour.

There is abroad today a mood of disenchantment and frustration because politics has disappointed us but ironically this mood may endanger such recovery of control as is open to us. Effective power is being gathered into relatively few hands. In this society where will the individual find confidence and self-reliance and a sense of responsibility? We face a dilemma in "the end of ideology," in the slipping of convictions about what can be achieved through politics, and this affects both governments, politicians and individuals. Answers to the many questions about human nature and society which this dilemma presents are not easy to find, but must be sought. The skill and power with which Principal Corry has marshalled the questions ensure our attention and concern.

J. A. CORRY, a distinguished political scientist, is a graduate of the University of Saskatchewan, Oxford and Columbia. He has been Professor of Law at the University of Saskatchewan, and Professor of Political Science at Queen's University, where he subsequently was appointed Vice-Principal, and, in 1961, Principal. He is the author, among other works, of *Democratic Government and Politics,* which, with the collaboration of J. E. Hodgetts, is now in its third edition.

Alan B. Plaunt Memorial Lectures
Carleton University, Ottawa, March 28, 30, 1963

THE
CHANGING
CONDITIONS
OF
POLITICS

J. A. CORRY

Published in co-operation with Carleton University
by University of Toronto Press

© University of Toronto Press 1963
Reprinted in paperback 2015
ISBN 978-1-4426-3941-6 (paper)

ALAN B. PLAUNT MEMORIAL LECTURES

I

IT IS BEING SAID nowadays, with some point, that this is a bad time for politicians. It is also a bad time for the students of affairs, sometimes called, without strict accuracy, political scientists. Some years ago, when I still rated myself in this category, I said that my subject, the study of politics, was being whittled away by theology at the one end and by sociology at the other. The remark was a pleasantry, and not an apt figure of speech.

I was not intending to say that others were poaching on our preserves. I really meant that political studies could no longer be confined to the frame many of us had thought adequate, that the field, as we had conceived it, did not bring nearly enough relevant matter under consideration. Further, I meant that we were not working in sufficient depth, either in the realm of theory or in our analysis of political institutions and political behaviour. I was admitting that sociologists and theologians and philosophers were more at home than we in some of the wider areas needing to be considered, and in some sections of the field had better tools for probing in depth.

In these admissions, I should take care not to speak for all political scientists but only for the majority who staked the field more narrowly and took a restricted view of what was directly relevant for political analysis. There have always been others who did not accept such limitations and pioneered in breadth and depth. (I add that with a few reservations conceded to a native skepticism, I belonged to the majority). Further, I should like to make clear that, in saying what I shall say in these lectures, I am not proposing an assignment in bankruptcy but rather arguing that the old firm needs to be re-organized in the light of new political realities that cannot be ignored.

What I meant some years ago can be said now with greater particularity and emphasis. First, the elements of human nature that were generally thought relevant for politics were too few and too simple to be adequate for basing political ideas and theories in our present situation. The view of human nature to which I refer was an optimistic one derived from the 18th century. Man was believed to be essentially rational and respectful of the claims of his fellows, acting in "general honest thought and common good to all." He was moved also by self-interest but the elements were so mixed in him as to ensure a basic nobility and goodness. Endowed with reason and a general disposition to the good, he could be trusted with a general freedom. Given the right conditions in which to exercise his reason and freedom, he could make of his life and society something nearly as fair as his best dreams. Free him from superstition and give him knowledge; free him from outmoded custom, arbitrary government and odious privilege, and give him equality of opportunity. In such a setting, no limits should be placed on the possibilities of human progress.

These ideas were perhaps adequate enough for the purposes in hand in the age of individualism and of liberal optimism that first stirred in the 16th century and matured in the 18th century, when only a small part of life was politicized. They were only partial insights, and they diverted attention from aspects of man that now bear on politics in a collectivist society (some would say mass society) where government intervenes deeply in everything and so brings a far more complex human response. The political ideas and theries which were based on these insights and which formed the staple of political debate and shaped the pattern of political events and institutions for so long have lost much of their power to stir us. More than that, events in the world at large have taken an alarming turn in the last generation for which the rationalist theories had not prepared us and for which they provide no satisfying explanation.

This, of course, is where the theologians come in. For the most part, they have always held to a more pessimistic and, in some respects, a more penetrating estimate of human nature. From their vantage point of the necessary imperfections of the finite, they have always put emphasis on sides of human nature that liberal rationalism has discounted too heavily. Holding that human destiny is not entirely amenable to the rational faculties, they have stressed the distractions of self-interest and self-love which can prostitute reason. They have been keenly aware of the depths of human nature where anxiety and fear generate malice and evil.

The clear-headed among the liberal rationalists have never denied the reality of egoism, malice and evil. The very existence of superstition, privilege and tyranny were proof of their pervasiveness and strength. In laying their bets on the goodness of man, they were really preferring to trust the generality of men rather than an oligarchy of entrenched and obscurantist authority. Nevertheless, having placed their money, they stressed the best qualities of their entry in the race and thus passed on to us an incomplete picture of human nature. The theologians have put stress on the other side: their estimates have clear relevance for the understanding of our times.

Since this is not an assignment in bankruptcy, I am not required to attribute failure to original sin or any other cosmic plight. In the perspective of time as distinct from eternity, other factors mould human behaviour, if not the deep essence of human nature, which may have bred the events for which we were unprepared and which our traditional political theories can no longer vitally engage.

This brings me to a second venture in particularizing. In confining intensive study and analysis, as we have in the past, to the essentially political phenomena, the organization and operation of governments, political parties and so on, political scientists have not taken enough account of the immense influence that the social structure as a whole exerts on political behaviour and on the movement of politics. In the age of individualism, perhaps this was justified. For a long time, political action through governments barely rippled the surface of the deeper reaches of society. Indeed, political *laissez faire* permitted the scientific and economic revolution of the past two centuries to work a profound revolution in the social structure, creating our collectivist society.

The collectivist society has generated new kinds of human behaviour, if indeed it has not created new kinds of men. Only when the social revolution was well advanced did government begin to intervene drastically in society. Government now penetrates and moulds almost every aspect of society, and it is inevitable that social forces should in turn react strongly on governments and politics. Students of politics and practising politicians have to cope with much more than the specifically political institutions, with much more than overt, specifically political, behaviour. Politics now has to do with all aspects of the social structure, and that is where the sociologists come in.

Because of lack of competence, I cannot offer here the kind of analysis that the theologian and the sociologist would give. I shall try not to "out talk my information" in a presumptuous way. I shall try to bring into relief some of the developments and current perplexities seen in one form or another in the United States and Britain as well as in Canada and fairly described as changing conditions of politics. I think our present perplexity is of the order described in an aphorism of Thurman Arnold "Unhappy is the nation that has run out of words to explain what is going on." So in the rest of this lecture I shall talk about the difficulties of understanding our present-day political world with the stock of political ideas and theories hitherto usually relied on for the purpose. In the second lecture, I shall look at some aspects of the collectivist society and consider how far these may be producing new dimensions in political behaviour. At this eleventh hour on the eve of April 8th,* it would be much better if I could say, with the cautious novelist hiding from the law of libel, that all parties and countries adverted to are entirely fictitious and any resemblance to existing parties and countries is purely coincidental. Because I cannot do that, I shall speak with as much detachment from the current scene as I can.

The age of individualism had revealed its main features by the 17th century. It matured, according to its nature, to form the liberal democratic age in the 19th century. Its constant aim was to tame the state. After the middle of the 19th century, it took up the supplementary purpose of making the state the sure instrument of the people. Irresponsible political power was taken to be the prime evil of the mundane world. It yielded little to law while it supported indefensible social privilege, and so was the root of all injustice and oppression. The remedy was to replace the reign of monarchs with the reign of law, and to make everyone equal under the

*These lectures were delivered at the end of March, 1963.

law. This would secure freedom for all under laws that all must obey.

The main technique for getting this happy result was extension of the franchise and the enlargement of the powers of popularly elected bodies and persons. Universal franchise was demanded in the sanguine hope that thereafter all the laws would be for the good of all. Although there were always some who knew better, it was widely believed that in the regime of freedom under laws made in the name and under the authority of all, social and economic deficiencies and injustices would, for the most part, melt away.

Early in the 20th century, formal freedom and formal equality under the law were achieved for all in Western Europe and North America. But formal freedom in itself did little to relieve basic poverty. Large sections of the population were still denied any effective meaningful freedom. The grossness of material inequality showed little sign of retreat. The continuing evils were now charged to *laissez faire*, the leeway that freedom gives to the unscrupulous and the ruthless as well as to the energetic, the single-minded and the toughly disciplined. Assaults on *laissez faire* began early in the 20th century with the emphasis in political aim shifting from freedom to equality or, more correctly, to the substantial reduction of inequality through use of the power of the state. Effort moved from political reform to social reform through political action.

Laissez faire, in the sense of a dominant theory determining public policy, was finally routed in the nineteen-thirties. But the social reformers who thus triumphed in a succession of battles from 1900 on over those who cherished the past whether from self-interest, fear, or scruple, split into socialists and liberal reformers, using the latter term (correctly I think) to cover both liberals and conservatives from 1930 on.

The socialists, in fiery revulsion against the indignity of mass unemployment and of poverty in the midst of plenty, were fortified in their long-standing conviction that meaningful freedom and social equality could only be gained by socializing the means of production and distribution. They had a passionate conviction of the essential goodness of man. They were sure that the capacity of man for generosity, compassion, co-operation and high endeavour was being stifled by capitalism. They were sure that all these qualities would blossom in a socialist society.

Strongly influenced by liberal democracy in which tradition they stand, they chose constitutional, parliamentary means to bring about the socialist society. They determined to capture the state through persuasion of the electorate and to make the government the official receiver of the entire estate of the bankrupt capitalist system. They confidently hoped to end injustice and inequality by nationalizing industry, and adopting comprehensive measures of social security. They engaged to guarantee order, stability and coherence by over-all social and economic planning, which thus became the most majestic function of government. Somehow, this programme was going to add economic democracy to political democracy, release all the generous and co-operative instincts, and realize the dream of effective freedom and social equality.

To the right of the socialists were ranged the older parties whom I have labelled reformers because they acknowledged that capitalism needed some reforming. Despite the tribulations of the free economy, they were confident of its resilience. They counted on it to reach new high levels of productivity which under proper contrivance would greatly narrow social inequalities. But where contrivance for equality seemed to threaten to submerge individual freedom, they were for freedom as the precious key to all social advance.

The great debate over these issues raged throughout the thirties. It was muted, if not suspended, by war and recovery from war in the forties. Modern war, of course, is a great socializer: the war of 1939–45 laid the foundations for a comprehensive system of social security by bringing into existence a steeply progressive tax structure. It extended the grip of government on economic life, a grip it has never really relinquished. In Britain, a socialist government between 1945 and 1951 kept up the socializing momentum of war, nationalizing large sections of industry and completing a great structure of social security. Even in the United States and Canada, without aid of socialist governments, the welfare state came to be accepted. A mixed economy emerged, neither socialist nor capitalist: motored, if you like, by private enterprise but levered and controlled, if not directed, by government.

A goodly part of the democratic socialist objectives was reached by the early fifties, although without nearly enough socialization of industry to satisfy doctrinaire prescriptions. One might have expected a redoubling of socialist energies to round out the programme. In fact,

however, socialists never recovered their old fire and conviction after the war. Of course, much that they had
argued for had been accepted, but they could well have
reviled it as being done in the wrong way and for the
wrong reasons.

Other factors also weakened the socialists. By lending
their weight to reform and so lightening social injustice,
they weakened their own fighting arm. Much of their
popular support rested on discontent and near-despair,
and it fell away as material conditions improved sharply.
Substantial numbers of workers, seeing the way open to
ascent in the social scale, became climbers, aspired to the
middle class, and actually acquired something of a bour-
geois style of life.

But there is more to it than all this. Many socialists
have become uncertain where they really want to go.
They are plagued by doubts rising from experience. In
the Soviet Union, freedom did not broaden down from
precedent to precedent as many had hoped. In fact, in
every country where government became fully master
and planned people's lives, frightful things were done.
Socialists, genuinely concerned for the essential freedom
of the human spirit, found themselves pondering more
anxiously than before Lord Acton's dictum that all
power corrupts.

There came to be more doubt too about the positive
gains to be set against the dangers in the exercise of
massive governmental power. The workers in the
nationalized industries of Britain did not feel any
freer, and were scarcely more grateful to, or more co-
operative with, the new socialist, than with the old

capitalist, management. All idealism suffers in its exposure to hard reality. The dream is never realized in all its purity. After six years of socialist government in Britain, so many things remained unbettered if not unchanged. Disenchantment set in and spread to the faithful in Canada and the United States.

The doubts have loosened the grip on doctrine. Revisionism, the disease that has always threatened socialist unity, waters down programmes until it appears that socialist parties are becoming middle class parties just as the working class, under the softening effect of prosperity and the welfare state, is becoming middle class in habit and aspiration. The burning conviction that once fired both leaders and followers does not glow as before.

The ideas and theories that fed the convictions are either accepted and absorbed into the consensus, or tried and found wanting, or filed away as too dangerous to be put to the touch. Not sure any more how to make a new society, socialist parties incline to think the present society might be nearly all right if they could get a chance to run it and put in a few new features. As someone said recently in Britain ". . . to try to alter the structure of British society by means of the British Labour Party is to surf-ride on two inches of water at ebb tide." Whatever else may be found to rouse generous socialist passion again, one can be pretty sure it will not be the ideas and theories that served in the recent past.

If socialist parties are "fresh out" of ideas, the parties to the right of them are even worse off. Such of them as have marched under the banner of reform in the last half century, have reached their objectives, seen their main programme put into force. Such of them as have been reluctant or opposed to the dominant political trends of the twentieth century may be still doubtful of where we are going but they cannot muster enough conviction to offer leadership in retreat from positions they fear to be untenable. The conservative reaction of the last decade, of which we have heard so much, has really been a movement of intellectuals. Its leaders have not been able to sell their doctrine to political parties on the democratic right. I suspect this is because their ideas do not appear to have any clear relevance to the political situation. No one can discern a line of retreat that is politically practicable.

So we seem almost to have reached the point where there is nothing to fight for, and nothing to fight against. This is not literally true. In the vast range of affairs within the ambit of governmental action, there are hundreds of issues on which political parties can take up opposing positions, more for housing and less for hospitals, old age pensions to be raised by $15.00 or $20.00, and so on almost endlessly. But arguments on such points are less than fascinating to the politically conscious members of the electorate, and do not nourish solid political conviction. Tension has largely disappeared from politics and we have gone slack.

In all this, there is nothing about which I should want to reproach the politicians or the political parties. We are not suffering from failure or bankruptcy but, it may well be, from the very magnitude of our success. It is worthwhile to pause and look at the scale of the achievement. In the countries under discussion, destitution has been ended, social inequalities greatly narrowed, and social security cushions provided against the major risks of an uncertain life. We have curbed economic exploitation and given dignity to labour insofar as mass production methods will allow. We have established economic equilibrium (still tenuous perhaps) in a mixed economy. Perhaps we have not abolished capitalism but we have changed it into something that neither its enemies nor its supporters in the early years of the century would recognize. We have done all this without either the civil war or the revolution which we were told so confidently a generation ago would be inevitable. We have done it without damaging the underlying consensus on which all democratic institutions depend. Indeed, we have enlarged the consensus and brought firmly within it most of the things I have been enumerating. Considering the millions of persons involved and the complexity of their affairs, this must be one of the high political achievements of history. Perhaps we are just dizzy from success.

At least it is true that the wide scope and firmness of the consensus has narrowed the front of the political struggle and brought it down, for the time being at least, from the realms of high strategy to the muddy ground of minor tactics where the fighting arm is not the flashing cavalry of ideas but the grubby sappers of inconsequential salients.

At any rate, we are disenchanted and we are asking why. Is it that the threat of the nuclear holocaust that hangs over us has paralyzed initiative in our domestic affairs? Is it that the aims of conservatives, liberals, socialists, the lot, have been too much focused on material improvement to be satisfying to the human spirit when immediate material needs are largely met? Does lurking puritanism in us give us an uneasy conscience as we come close to wallowing in abundance? Or is it, as Justice Holmes thought, that life needs to be a roar of bargain and battle, and not to have the roar is a bore? Does life get its savour from uncertainty and peril which we might just barely overcome if we committed all our powers and faculties to the effort? Do we miss "the gaunt troops mustering in the grisly dawn"? In short, why do we lie in the doldrums taking no pride in our political achievements?

I do not pretend to have answers to these questions. None of them can be asked seriously without acknowledging the possibility that man is something other, or more, than most of the rationalist liberal theories and ideas about politics have assumed him to be. Put more precisely, the question is whether elements of human nature that we thought could be left out of account in political calculation now have to be counted as engaged in the political process. This, by the way, should not be surprising. Politics now cuts deeply into everybody's life and social relationships and can be expected to evoke a fuller and much more varied response. It is even possible, as I shall suggest in the next lecture, that drastic changes in the social structure are producing a new kind of man, or at least bringing hitherto latent potentialities of the creature into overt expression.

Leaving all that aside for the moment, some suggestions may be ventured. The long struggle to reduce inequalities in the distribution of this world's goods was materialist enough in immediate aim, and for good reasons. Chill poverty froze the genial currents of the soul. When the means to mend the situation came to hand, failure to press them to that purpose would have been a gross form of injustice. But all the while it was dreamed that, if the curse could be lifted the spacious opportunities thus opened would lift spirits everywhere and we would soar beyond the confines of the material. We have begun to fear that this may not happen. On the evidence, we seem to be settling down to enjoy ourselves in the lap of comfort. The advertisers give us soothing assurance that this is all we know, or need to know. Indeed, we have come to fear that our children learn more about the good life from the advertisers than from their teachers.

It surely does not overstate the case to say that life needs more purpose than can be found in taking our ease among our gadgets. The shiftlessness of much of our enjoyment leads to disquiet and boredom. Everywhere, we reproach ourselves for lack of standards, for the dearth of commitments beyond ourselves. The boredom extends to politics because we are unable to see how we can act politically to remedy this dearth and lack. The enrichment of life, the finding of purposes on which to spend ourselves, are essentially matters of individual commitment and action. They cannot be achieved by collective action. Collective action can create liberating opportunities. This we have been doing. But it cannot command performance to the measure of the opportunity. Because politics does not seem to open a way for what we most need, we become frustrated as well as bored with it. I know how risky it is to try to guess the minds of young people but I will hazard that this is a very widespread mood among them.

In Britain, in these days, there is much demand for a sense of national purpose to overcome admittedly widespread apathy. A recent Canadian book, in its title and its first two chapters, calls for a social purpose for Canada and documents our purposelessness. The bulk of the book, however, does not deal with purpose but only with the means of liberating opportunity through government policy. Getting a unified *social* purpose, collectively hitching ourselves to a star, is not an easy matter nor one to be taken up lightly.

As far as I know, democratic governments have not been able to gear themselves to a unified social purpose except in time of war. In the aim of winning a war, government finds ready-made an overriding purpose which is generally approved. As we know, this purpose or objective is used to submerge for the time being many of the diverse and conflicting purposes of individuals and groups. Government establishes firm priorities among the claims and demands that come up spontaneously from below. It goes further, and brushes aside, if it does not crush, the reservations and resistances of minorities.

Of course, there are satisfactions in this sense of unity of aim which frees us from the distraction of cross-purposes. There is exhilaration in marching together when none is for the party and all are for the state. Who has not yearned to find in time of peace a moral equivalent for war? Yet in our reflective moments, we know that such moods of exaltation do not last; indeed are only maintained at heavy psychic cost. When release from the tension of the forced march comes, the zest for undisciplined expression is almost pathological and could only be checked by severe repression.

Except in times of extreme peril generally recognized as such, a free society cannot take things at this pitch. Genuine freedom bears its fruit in diversity of aim and interest. Individuals and groups will try to do what they find good, and the pursuit brings them into collision and struggle. Liberal democratic government exists to compromise these clashes without civil war and not to infuse us all with a sense of national purpose.

Why then are we yearning for such a sense of purpose? Clearly because we think we are not, as a people, doing anything like justice to the possibilities that near-affluence has suddenly opened up for us. Until yesterday, so to speak, large sections of the population found an all-absorbing purpose in keeping the wolf from the door. With the marked easing of the grim pressure of poverty, relatively few of them find quickly alternative forms of self-discipline to absorb them. This should not be taken as a ground for condescension or puritanical criticism. Most of us have too much glass in our houses to risk throwing stones.

Elevating and edifying purpose has never been a universal characteristic of the comfortable classes. But as long as the numbers in the comfortable classes were few, the volume of frivolity in our society seemed small and could be looked at indulgently. It is the sudden multiplying by hundreds of times of those who seem not to be steadied by self-imposed purpose that makes the impression of aimlessness so oppressive, and brings us as close to a sense of sin as a sceptical generation can come.

We are wanting a sense of national purpose, and are distressed not to be able to articulate it in our politics. We have come to expect governments to fix up whatever is wrong, without recognizing that it is one thing for governments to remove barriers and obstructions to the good life and quite another to ensure that the good life will be lived at a high pitch. Some of the vitality of initiative in our social life has weakened in the last 30 years. I shall try to suggest reasons for this in the next lecture.

It is time to worry about a society when initiative does not well up from below in a diversity of demands and aims that keeps governments hard at work to reconcile. If we need to be set on fire—as I think we do—what is needed is a renewal of zest and dash all through our society and not mandates to governments to find purposes and then bind us to them.

Another set of changes in our circumstances is of great significance. In the course of reaching consensus on the mixed economy and the welfare state, we have created an economic and political structure of great complexity. The steadily accelerating spread of large scale enterprise and organization has removed large sectors of the economy from the dictates of the market.

As the self-regulating capacity of the economy declined, governmental regulation advanced to cover the deficiency. This in turn diminished still further that self-regulating capacity. Economic life is now governed by a mixture of private decisions taken in the corporate sector of the economy and of public decisions taken by the governments with the latter constantly assuming greater importance. Whether or not the aim is confessed, the gropings of governments in relation to economic policy are designed now to get a good measure of integrated planning under government auspices. The result is towering economic organization, massive governmental structure and an extremely complex interlocking of relationships between them. We find all this extremely bewildering.

We know our duty as citizens to understand the complexities. The liberal individualistic belief over three centuries has been that men, by taking thought, could control their destinies. We have plenty of examples around us showing what happens when massive power, economic, political or whatever, gets out of control. Yet if we propose alteration of policy in a way that seems eminently sensible or strike out at action that seems outrageous to the fair-minded, we soon find we are tearing at a seamless web; and the thing we want to move will involve moving many other things as well, some of them, as like as not, things we cherish. We come to see that government policy as a whole finds an equilibrium, not by applying the full logic of clear and lovely ideas but by a series of compromises of a variety of groups, all mobilized to defend their interests.

We have little confidence that the infinitesimal weight of our vote in periodic elections will do much to modify the pattern of governmental action. Attempts to force a modification of the pattern in any other way require the pressure of highly organized groups brought to bear at the precisely right time and place. The existing equilibrium is defended against attack, not so much because of its merits (although they will be loudly proclaimed) but because even minor shifts in adjustment in one sector of public policy are likely to have widespread and, to some extent, unforeseeable consequences in other sectors. It is indeed too delicate to be exposed to any tinkering that can be resisted, and patterns of governmental action and expenditure sometimes persist even when they are no longer defensible.

The citizen is tempted to conclude that as government action brings more and more aspects of his life and affairs within its orbit, he is being progressively stripped of effective influence on its direction. Of course, he would be wrong so to conclude. Individuals, standing alone, have rarely had any significant political influence on central, as distinct from local, governments. But that is almost beside the point. The waning of confidence in the political process does not rest on judgments about the facts but on a general feeling of remoteness from it all. Control over what government does seems to pass into fewer and fewer hands, a relatively small coterie of political leaders, higher civil servants, and spokesmen for tightly organized interests.

So we reach the concept of the establishment, a notion that has had much derisive elaboration in Britain and covers the insiders of one kind or another who seem to have taken our destiny out of our hands. Most significantly, the establishment is now often defined as including such political leaders now out of power and organized interests presently out of favour as are likely to come to power and favour at the next turn of the wheel. Even if they are not possessing our birthright at the moment, it is thought that they soon will be, and therefore they fall under the same odium. In this mood, we flirt with movements that have not yet incurred the odium, imagining mistakenly that somehow it will be in their power and interest to restore to us something we feel we have lost. Short of destroying the consensus we have reached, the politico-economic structure calls for political power to be exercised much as it has been exercised in the past fifteen years.

Ironically, the mood of disenchantment and frustration that arises because politics has disappointed us endangers such recovery of control over our destiny as is open to us. Given the decisive influence of government policy on our economic and social arrangements, it is, of course, vital that government should be firm and resolute, yielding only the minimum to dispersive pressures. The only likely way to secure such government is to have a reasonably well disciplined party system in command of parliament.

The range of government action is so wide and affects everyone in so many diverse ways that a welter of issues confuses every election. The voter finds himself drawn to one party on one issue and repelled on another. The old simplicities like Home Rule for Ireland, Free

Trade, Dominion Status are gone, and none with such deceptive clarity has taken their place. The mood of irritation clouds the vision still further and takes as its object precisely the political parties that have pressed discipline on parliament as well as limited our leverage on our representatives there. For these are the two faces of the same coin.

In the world of big organization in which we, as individuals, are now bundled and jammed, the main hope for combining coherence and stability with responsible criticism and orderly adjustment of economic and social life is to submit to still other big organizations, the political parties that can be counted on to create majorities in parliament at one time or another. In this country at least, the changing conditions of politics raise doubts about the ability of the party system to create such majorities.

I said earlier that the Anglo-American countries had made a great achievement in reaching a broad consensus on the mixed economy and the welfare state. Taken by itself, this tends to confirm the more optimistic view of the nature of man as it bears on politics. Men moved by "general honest thought and common good to all" would, of course, be likely to come to such a consensus.

Yet, to our surprise, hard on the heels of this achievement, new dimensions in our politics seem to open. Perhaps all we need is time to take our bearings, and then the circumstances and moods that puzzle us will pass. Not having foreseen that we would come to this point, perhaps we should not take too seriously the fact that we do not see how we are to get away from it. Periods of hesitation in the life of a society are not at all unusual. However, there is a view that we are confronted by much more than political ripples on the surface of society. It is held that profound social changes that have been going on for a long time are forcing their way into politics and contributing strongly to the hesitations, moods, and attitudes I have spoken about. This possibility will be considered in the next lecture.

II ▪▬▬▬▬▬▬▬▬▬▬▬▬▬▬▬▬▬▬▬▬▬▬▪

HERE I shall speak mainly about the relationship of the individual to society. Much of the debate on this subject assumes that individual and society must always be in conflict. Actually, such talk is scarcely older than the seventeenth century. In the Middle Ages, man's consciousness of himself was always social. He thought of himself as a member of an organic group, be it a family, feudal manor, guild, corporation or parish. Not until the Renaissance and Reformation did he think of himself as a detached entity, separate from society, and so, potentially at least, in conflict with it.

The sixteenth century ushered in the age of individualism in whose twilight we still live. For reasons we need not enter into here, some men became intoxicated with the possibilities of individual freedom and rebelled against the social restraints of immemorial custom, church and government. From this impulse came by stages all the freedoms we have known and celebrated, freedom to think beyond the boundaries of the socially approved wisdom, economic freedom from the restraints of manor, guild and government decree, political freedom from the rule of dynasties and monarchs.

The individual became the fundamental premise for political theory. Man, the individual, is born free. He is the basic datum of nature. Society and government are artifices designed to serve the individual. He is primary, and all social arrangements secondary and derived. All social bonds are open to criticism and to dissolution if they do not serve the aims and needs of the individual.

The sanguine liberal view of the eighteenth and nineteenth centuries regarded the individual as essentially good, depreciated social restraints and urged an almost anarchic freedom. John Stuart Mill, in the essay *On Liberty* argued that a man's freedom should only be restricted when his actions threatened definite and assignable harm to other men. Indeed, with *laissez faire* effectively keeping the hands of government off individuals in his day, Mill thought the most obnoxious restraints on freedom were those imposed by society through custom rather than by the state through law. The individual was set in opposition to society and thought to be in perennial conflict with it.

We got into this way of thinking because it took so long to emancipate the individual, to break the authority of long-standing social custom fortified by religious taboos and to throw off the burden of mercantilism and other indefensible privileges maintained by the state. The enormous reservoirs of energy and initiative released at each stage of the freeing of the individual seemed to show that he was indeed the key to progress. He was the indestructible entity whose nobility consisted in standing for himself by himself. Free him from the social shackles that had bound him in the past, and the future was illimitable.

Of course, the individual has never been able to stand by himself but has always had to be buoyed up by social supports. Individuals as persons always emerge with the stamp of a social matrix on them. The very structure of an individual's personality arises from the particular network of social relationships in which he is enmeshed. How else would we get the rich variety of identifiable types and styles of persons? The family from which a person comes and the community in which he shares contribute not only to his queerness but to his preferences, his demeanour in success and adversity, his stock of stability, integrity and fortitude, in fact his whole character. All this we know without access to the case studies of the psychiatrists.

Modern individualism is a product of Western Europe. The original inspiration for it came from men nurtured in mediaeval society which itself was marked by a uniquely rich community life. The manorial village, the guild, the local corporation, the free city, the parish, the monastery and the religious orders gave status to their members, bound them together in protective association, and provided social supports of a remarkable, even if confining and restrictive, order. The revolutionary changes of the sixteenth century shattered some of these forms of community, transformed others, and sowed the seeds of some new ones. With the breaking of these moulds, individualism got its chance. But it got its chance in a society that still retained many vital forms of group and community life. At the least, there continued in vigour and good repair, from the sixteenth century on to the nineteenth, the family, the parish, the village, and a range of self-sufficient districts and small regions that produced identifiable types of men, and gave them a sense of belonging as they tried, or were forced to try, to carry the role of the free self-directing individual. In North America, essentially similar patterns of community were created out of imitation or need, or both.

For the most part, these communities had a unity from which many, although by no means all, of their members drew strength. They were not as tightly knit as the mediaeval communities. There was more movement in and out of them and much less sense of the corporate responsibility of the group for the welfare of its members. As economic life broke free from the earlier social and religious restraints, the weak and unfortunate often went down into destitution as the strong went up. Individualism always had high costs and these rose sharply as the Industrial Revolution got under way.

Nevertheless, the family, the village, town, district, were generally economic and social units, more or less self-sufficient, in which many individuals could see themselves as carrying significant functions and sharing significantly in a common life. The parish and the church not only ministered to spiritual needs but also provided material succour and welfare. Most of the conditions of life were set within these boundaries, and so the members of the community understood them and could try to cope with them. Even when their members were divided into social classes, these communities were simple in structure, and face-to-face relationships eased the acerbities of class feeling. Individuals readily understood their places in them, and got a sense of belonging to a vital functioning community. In family, church and local community, the indispensable supports for individualism were found.

Venturesome individuals were always moving out of them into the wider world where they often appeared convincingly as free individuals standing alone and making their way without visible social supports. Whether they stayed at home or went afield, they had been formed and shaped and the structures of their personalities set by the local community. They often thought of themselves as being in revolt against the community that had shaped them. Yet, they were, in the truest sense, its product, individuals formed in the matrix of their particular community.

From the beginning of the nineteenth century, this social structure began to break down, and it has gone on crumbling ever since at different rates for different countries and regions, but always at an accelerating pace. The primary causes, of course, were the unleashing of individual initiative from social restraints, the releasing of inventiveness, the development of transport and communications. Economic freedom led to expanding trade and a growing articulation of the free market for goods and labour. These, in turn, promoted division of labour and specialized production. Then came newer and still more effective machines, new forms of power, bigger units of production, the assembly line, giant corporations, vast industrial cities, all in breath-taking rapidity in some 150 years.

The economic outcome of this is the highly integrated industrial structure with concentration of control of the critical sectors of it in large, and often huge, corporations. To be able to match the corporations, trade unions must reach for size and power. Other participants in economic life try to organize, by one means or another, on a comparable scale. The free market which used to determine the movement of prices and allocate the factors of production no longer conducts the economic orchestra but takes a subordinate and supporting role. Instead, more and more of the basic critical decisions are made by, or at least in the name of, big organizations, corporations, trade unions, and trade associations with or without the stimulus, pressure, admonition or direction of governments.

The social outcome is the massing of people in sprawling urban confusion. Few persons in these cities are their own masters in their own work. For the most part, they are employees working under direction at highly specialized tasks, more or less infected by dull mechanical routine. The daring and resourceful entrepreneur of an earlier day has been succeeded by the organization man.

I said that the older social structure typical of the modern age until the late nineteenth century has been crumbling under the stress of these developments. To the eye, many of the elements of that structure are still visible, but the independent vitality they once exhibited has been greatly weakened. The family persists and still is central to the lives of many people, but speaking generally it has lost much of its tight unity and sense of corporate responsibility for its members as they spend their day in occupations remote from it and merely come home to sleep. The local community, whether village, town or countryside with its focus in neighbourhood institutions of school and church, is still there in profusion, but its relative self-sufficiency and sense of close identity have largely gone. The basic reason for this has been the industrial and the technological revolution of the last 150 years.

Increasingly, and at different paces in different countries through the nineteenth century, and into the twentieth century, the magnetic pull of distant markets drew more and more of the energies of these communities into specialized production for those markets. In time, they were nearly all drawn into deep dependence on a continued demand for their products in far-away places, and so exposed to events quite beyond their control and still further beyond their understanding. Finally caught up on a national and even international exchange of goods and services, they lost most of their self-sufficiency and independence, and the vitality of these social supports of individuals was sapped away.

In the great industrial cities, to which vast numbers have been drawn out of the small towns and countryside, generation after generation, the populations have never known any significant self-sufficiency or enjoyed any effective individual independence. Most of them are irretrievably committed to employment at specialized jobs and thus heavily dependent on economic events and decisions beyond their ken and control. Except for subsistence farmers on the fringes, we have all been enticed far out on the limbs of interdependence where we may be sawed off any time by the almost whimsical chances of economic change.

When large sections of the nation got drawn into this order of interdependence and found themselves racked by economic change, or economic growth, or whatever you want to call it, the vulnerable specialists of every kind were driven to beg for the intervention of the state. The government was implored by the victims of economic change, and by the comfortable people with social consciences, to regulate the economy, to compensate for its swings and shifts, and to cushion individuals against the misfortunes they were unable to ward off by their own actions. In a very short time, almost before we knew it, we were drawn into the mixed economy and the welfare state. The growth of big organization in the private sphere was matched by the growth of big government.

Perhaps big government can regulate, compensate, stabilize and cushion. Given the economic and social structure we have, only two main ways are open. Government may dominate the private sphere completely by its edicts and plan our lives comprehensively. Or it may secure close co-operation between itself and the private sector composed of corporate industrial and financial power, trade unions, organized agriculture, and so on. But in either case, a relatively few persons and small groups will make the decisions, taking somewhat into account the pressures and influences that play upon them. The intense intellectual effort that used to go into trying to understand the economic mysteries of the market is being steadily diverted into the study of the logic, psychology and sociology of decision-making. We know that decisions made somewhere by others than ourselves will be fateful for us all.

Effective power is being gathered into relatively few hands and face-to-face communities that might combat anonymity and restlessness have been enfeebled. If the individual personality is in large measure the product of the society in which it emerges, what kind of persons can this society be expected to produce? If stalwart individuality always has to be underpinned by social supports, what trusswork of the present social structure will serve? Where do people, for whom vital decisions are made without their sharing in them in any meaningful way, learn a sense of responsibilty for themselves and their actions? Where people are always conscious of dependence on hidden events beyond their reach and control, how do they escape the pathological worries and anxieties which can only be kept at bay by assurances of security from the cradle to the grave? Will there be any enthusiasm for a wide personal freedom in which the risks and responsibilities seem incommensurate with the foreseeable gains and advantages?

I do not ask these questions for rhetorical effect but because I do not think answers to them can be given with any confidence. Of course, there is a very close relationship between the personality structure and the structure of society. Yet it would be rash to say that personality is merely a function of the social structure. For example, the decline in the firmness and intensity of religious belief weakens the obligation felt to resist social pressures and take the burden of individual freedom and responsibility. Certainly, the conviction that one will have to answer at the judgment seat for one's witness in the world here below has, in the past, stiffened the demand for individual freedom because freedom was needed to get ready to face that awful responsibility. Yet a vital religion has to bind together the fragments of knowledge and experience in an interpretation that makes sense of that knowledge and experience. The great advance of knowledge and the changes in society in the last two centuries were certain to provoke the radical reassessment of religious beliefs and values that has been going on for a long time now. While it is going on, some of the older religious certainties are under suspended sentence, to say the least. So it is not clear to me that the weakening of specific religious conviction is any more cause than it is consequence in the complex of relationships under discussion.

At any rate, the dominant patterns of our social life are no longer individualistic but collectivist in the sense that groups and closely knit organizations, instead of individuals, are the units of decision and action. Physically, a great part of the population is massed in urban areas. By occupation and material interest, they are massed as wage or salary employees, members of trade unions or similar associations. Politically, attempts are made, sometimes with success, to mass them for election purposes. The entertainment industry tries to mass them for its spectacles which are cooked up for what are believed to be the mass tastes. There is much talk about mass society, and about mass man who takes supinely the proffered standards of his society and responds predictably to stimuli that move the great bulk of his fellows.

We are being told too about the alienation of the mass man. Marx first gave currency to the concept of alienation as the estrangement of the exploited worker from the satisfactions of creative work as he worked for a capitalist employer. The concept has now been extended to include estrangement of the individual from any satisfying form of identity with a community, and even from himself as an effective human person. The social analysts of today, who are not studying decision-making, are studying mass society, mass man, and alienation.

Even if I had the competence, there is not time here to spell out in long hand, as it were, the analysis for which these words are the shorthand. In the briefest terms, the weakening of older primary forms of community and the failure to replace them with enough new and vital forms of association leave the individual insecure, unfulfilled, frustrated and alone with the terrifying burden of consciousness. If this conclusion is right, our present time is more individualistic than any the modern world has known. But the atomized individual of today, it is said, is not the confident, self-reliant person, cherishing his freedom and distinctiveness, that

we have idealized for so long. He cannot find a focus
for vital individual expression in mechanized work
whose dull routines have little meaning for him. Nor
can he find it in impersonal consumption of standardized
products. In his hunger to belong somewhere, he seeks
shared experience in standardized entertainments and
mass spectacles. In his rootlessness, he becomes the mass
man.

At the same time, many vital decisions affecting the
average individual's life are removed from any forum
in which he can take a direct and effective part. Economic and political centralization reduces the number
of persons who set the main terms of existence and
entangles the deliberations in expert and technical considerations which he cannot follow, even if he knows
where and by whom matters are being settled. "The
area of individual action, decision and responsibility
shrinks in favour of collective planning and decision."
In this sense, society becomes collectivist and the collective institutions that have, to a marked degree, sup-
planted the older forms of community do not integrate
individuals in them in a vital way.

Individuals, conscious of their vulnerability and dependence, and aware of the need for authority somewhere to hold together the parts of the vast interde-
pendent structure of present-day society, cease to feel
any deep responsibility for what goes on. They acquiesce
in, if they do not actively push for, extension of government action and direction. People listen resignedly to
politicians who assure them that, given power, they will
do what is needed to integrate the society and protect

its members from the mischances of rapid economic and social changes. The power and scope of the state grow with great rapidity. The social forces that formerly acted as a check on the state decline in strength and this decline raises sharply the question how excessive concentration of power in the state is to be prevented. In this analysis, the vulnerable individual and the all-powerful state are two sides of the same coin.

It is very hard to say how far the emerging social realities prefigure the alarming features of the mass man and the all-powerful state. Social causation is the most complex of all studies even when we are looking at clearly defined, fully shaped phenomena. We have not that advantage—or disadvantage—here. The most that the prophets of the mass man say is that he is coming, the type is emerging, and that dangerously large numbers of persons in urban industrial areas exhibit more or fewer of his features. Equally, it is not yet seriously urged by many that the state is really out of control but rather that it is moving rapidly in that direction.

Of course, there are substantial numbers of rootless people who feel that society does not provide them opportunities for a meaningful existence and who fail to establish any satisfying relationship with vital social groups. There have always been numbers of these, even when the older forms of primary community were going at their best. The issue really is the new strength of the tendencies, the proportion of the population seriously exposed to the tendencies, and how deeply disinherited their situation makes them feel. Measuring the disintegrative forces at work on millions of people is a delicate task in which the margin of error may well invalidate the findings.

The summary account given here of the factors driving towards mass society overlooks or skimps a number of important considerations. First, even in great industrial cities, neighbourhood institutions persist—or develop—giving many of the inhabitants some sense of mutuality and belonging. The fact that London can be described as a collection of villages illustrates the point. The massive national and international trade unions are among the large-scale organizations that dwarf the individual and help to form his impression of remoteness from significant decisions. This, however, is only part of the picture. Trade unions had their origins in friendly societies and mutual benefit societies in which industrial workers in the early nineteenth century tried to compensate for the loss of older forms of rural and village community. A multitude of trade union locals everywhere provide today some of the texture of community for their members, aside altogether from the better-known function of collective bargaining. Co-operatives, both producer and consumer, serve the same kind of ends.

Indeed, for at least 200 years, as people have felt the loosening of the older social bonds, they have tried to compensate for the loss by a wide scatter of voluntary associations. The Masonic Order, for example, came to life late in the eighteenth century and provided, for a long time, a quality of cohesion that was often alarming to governments. Countless other similar orders and fraternities have risen and fallen. While their life histories do not suggest enduring vitality, they do testify to the continuing effort to find a social meaning for existence.

The effort has intensified in our own day, if the number and variety of the voluntary associations that rise and flourish is a reliable index. In a great many of them, the bond is occupational and they become, if they do not begin as, political pressure groups. As such, their competition keeps up the tension of political life and contributes to an equilibrium that avoids extremes. However, being of the sappers rather than of the cavalry, they do little to elevate political discussion.

Moreover, the associations that aspire to weighty political influence need the weight of mass membership. As membership gets big, control of the higher activities of the association slips away from the rank and file into the hands of a few. The association becomes an aggravation rather than a mitigation of bigness, remoteness and anonymity.

Many of the groups formed on the basis of a common interest are devoid of political content. Membership in such as these may well constitute resignations from political involvement, thus releasing politicians from importunities. Unfortunately, a low level of political awareness cannot be a gain for liberal democracy because the unreflecting voter is the most vulnerable to demagogic appeal.

Nevertheless, all lively voluntary action in groups knits people into social textures. Where such groups flourish in abundance, they are checks on the emergence of mass man. A dictator always tries to crush voluntary associations because they are potential centres of opposition to him. He wants a mass society because he knows that its members will need him and will rise to his appeals. Quite independently of this fact, the evidence is clear that political extremism is in inverse ratio to the number and vitality of voluntary associations. The Anglo-American societies still have marked powers of resistance to the spread and deepening of the stain of alienation.

There are still other relevant considerations. Even within massive industry itself, which has long been a principal source of alienation, the numbers of jobs calling for a high degree of technical knowledge rise rapidly. Here, as elsewhere, knowledge can be power. The man who has the indispensable knowledge shares in decisions. Thus, both pride of competence and sense of responsibility are nurtured. The more his job calls upon him to think, the more he will want to think for himself. Automation will call for steadily rising proportions of the work force to have and to exercise educated judgment. Also, automated industries, not needing to be planted alongside large pools of labour, offer new chances for physical deconcentration that would lessen the mass tendencies always at work in the great cities. But whether the net effect of automation will be beneficial depends on what is done about the redundant workers it displaces. The alienated mass man at the extreme is the unemployed and unemployable derelict.

It needs also to be remembered that the response of individuals to their environment is affected by their level of education. As secondary education comes within the reach of most youngsters and as access to university education is greatly widened, we can talk, without wild inaccuracy, more about an educated society. An educated society will have more resources to resist alienation and the herd-like responses that characterize mass society.

Aside from all specific consolations, it must be kept in mind that these are times of rapid and dismembering change. Living by habit and custom as much as we can, we are most alert to the disintegrative which disturbs what we have known. Recuperative forces may go unrecognized because they appear in the repellent garb of the new.

Yet, when all the reservations have been made and all the cautions put, there is little doubt that the grain of mechanized industrial society runs towards regimentation and standardization. The rationalizing of processes and of organization argues for larger and larger organizations so that more things will be calculable and manageable at the top. Freedom and diversity always seem, on the surface at any rate, to make trouble for those charged with getting the gears to mesh. Compensating for this bias calls for awareness, energy, ingenuity and vigilance.

There is plenty of evidence that all these are needed. We are baffled to see juvenile delinquency rise despite the general rise in the standard of living. We could find the clue in the fact that juvenile delinquency is found at its worst, not in the countryside, not in the non-industrial community, but precisely in the urban industrial city. Youth is responsive to the immediate in its environment. So, it is tempting to conclude that family and neighbourhood ties are failing to satisfy the ache to belong somewhere. The most popular post-war philosophy for younger people is existentialism. Its basic appeal is the assertion that man is solitary and alone, alienated from the world. To save his dignity from abject complicity in the absurd, he must outface despair by acceptance and commitment to life without illusions. (Right or wrong, this calls for courage, and so is hopeful.) For a philosophy to get attention, it has to make sense in the experience of those who embrace it. If there was genuine rapport with inherited values and satisfaction in social relationships, young people would be affirming with animal spirits, if nothing else, and leaving disillusion and despair to the older and wiser.

Whether deep in disillusion and despair or not, much of the working force of today finds little that is exciting and satisfying in its work. For those caught up in mechanized work processes over which they have no significant control, unrest is never far around the corner. The attempt to make such work interesting has almost been given up. Instead, hopes are fastened on shorter hours so that people can find themselves in extended leisure. Play, recreation and amusement are heavy preoccupations today. Many of the offerings, however, are canned and packaged with little of spontaneous play or lively sharing in them. Do we conclude that, in the main, the tension of work is so wearing to the spirit that no mean between frenzy and passivity will serve? Anyway, at the best, the results so far are an indifferent return on the dreams about what release from unremitting toil would do.

Whether or not leisure so used restores the man to face his work, it adds little to his stature as a citizen. The counselling of mass advertising on the uses of leisure is no doubt thought to be fitted to its audience. If any of this advice suggests the raptures of study and reflection about public things, it has escaped me. Even after a heavy discount for the perennial puritan distaste for folk pleasures, the corrected judgment would still be bleak. The end of the urban work-day releases a jaded spirit wanting to be steeped in forgetfulness rather than an eager citizen hasting to the library or the forum. The serious issue thus posed is whether the fault is irremediably in ourselves or in the social and work environment that closes us in.

The likely effects of these social trends on politics can now be sketched. Individual freedom will not be as highly prized by men who lack the zest and the genuine opportunity to use it in their social and economic relations. If government is not seen as a baleful threat to opportunities they want to seize and can see ways of using, they will not be so vigilant to keep it in check. On the contrary, as the autonomy of the face-to-face communities and groups in which they live is eroded by social and economic change, they are led to put their trust in government rather than in themselves because government has the long reach that is needed and which they lack. At the least, in their anxiety and dependence, they are open to persuasion to that effect. The rule of law, for example, is not maintained, in the long pull, by courts, constitutions and bills of rights but by the citizen's passion for liberty. Bagehot made the point by saying that the men of Massachusetts could work any constitution. It is not likely that the mass society will produce that kind of men, even in Massachusetts.

It is said that men shirk responsibility. It is always a burden, and burdens are always irksome. In propitious times, they can be led to welcome responsibility because of compensating advantages seen to reside in freedom. But if effective power is denied one in one's own affairs, why play a game that one must always lose? Moreover, faculties rust if they do not shine steadily in use. If, in one's daily work, one does not think for one's self, weigh the pros and cons, decide on action, and abide the consequences, it is rather much to expect reasoned and responsible decision to be exercised intermittently in politics. Of course, there has never been a society in which the great bulk of the citizens was thus prepared for political participation. The essential point is that the fraction so habituated by their life-style and experience is declining sharply in our society. Most of us are employees of one kind or another.

At the very time when the attraction to, and the capacity for, participation in things public is diminishing, the sphere of things political moves to cover issues beyond our immediate experience. Because government has come to envelop a large part of our lives, the issues multiply and take on a forbidding perplexity. The clear-cut simple alternatives disappear. Instead of yes or no, the alternatives are often more or less. Deficit financing was wrong last year, but right this year, and so on. These are not the problems for jaded spirits to take up and judge.

In these circumstances, the politician will be driven to simplify and dramatize. How near to demagoguery he has to go to do this is open to dispute. At least, it is clear that, if the need of individuals to belong somewhere is not satisfied in the primary communities and in face-to-face relationships, they are all the readier to be taken, as crowds, into the emotionally charged fellowship of the nation. When moved in this way, they are not asserting their freedom and diversity as individuals but running for cover into the shelter of the state which can become a prison.

For whatever tendencies there are in this direction, I shall not be the one to blame the politician. Like every other artist, he is, in large measure, subdued by his materials. If his materials are crowds rather than a multiplicity of diverse and opposing wills and interests, he has to work in that medium. As soon as the crowd element is decisive, he will cease to be the democratic politician we know and become the charismatic leader.

The politician in a free society always has to face a wide range of conflicting interests and wills. The interests are clearly articulated as expressions of the desire for freedom of action and the belief in its possibilities. For the same reason, the wills are stubborn, and, left unmediated, would disrupt public order. The job of the democratic politician is to reconcile the conflicts by compromise in a policy that is tolerable to nearly all, even if congenial to few. To do his job, he needs room for manoeuvre. It must be open to him and his party to propose, and to carry through, changes of policy that meet the prime and indispensable need for reconciliation of conflicting interests and wills.

Here we come upon another significant feature of the changing conditions of politics. As the scope of state action has widened enormously and government has superseded the market in fixing many of the terms of economic and social activity, the freedom of action of the politician has correspondingly narrowed. In the complex interlocking of economic life, adjustments in one sector affect many other sectors. Everything is related to everything else. If stability is to be maintained and the hopes for economic growth realized, government has to pursue a set of interrelated policies which cannot be reshuffled with impunity. More than that, in the setting of the policies in the first place, and in any responsible adjusting and modifying of them, the likely effects have to be calculated.

Expert judgment is needed at every turn. The higher civil servants have to be relied on for the *expertise*, and they thus come to play a big part in the policy-making. To a degree, policy becomes bureaucratized and caught in the rigidities that always vex large-scale organization. So the politician is denied some of the flexibility he needs for working out his reconciliations. His room for manoeuvre is narrowed. In a sense, he too is alienated from his proper work and subject to frustrations.

The logic of the argument can be carried one step further. When the market really ruled, its decrees were inexorable. People were compelled to adjust themselves to it at whatever cost. We decided a long time ago that the human cost was much too high. We have deposed the market and are putting government in its place. Government decree may not be as pitiless as was that of the market but, if we are to maintain economic stability and nourish economic growth, it must have its own inexorability. Public policy cannot be adjusted to every need for political compromise. Accordingly, instead of adjusting policy to the people, it will be necessary, in considerable measure, to adjust the people to the policy. This feat does not call for the arts of the democratic politician but rather for the magic of the leader whose art is not so much reconciliation as submergence of wills and interests.

Clearly enough then, the mass tendencies in society and the transformed role of government work together to threaten drastic changes in our politics. They will continue so to work as long as the drive to large-scale organization and centralization of power seem to us the necessary conditions for ensuring rapid economic growth and for raising productivity. And we are all preoccupied with getting greater material means and distributing the benefits more widely for the relief of man's estate.

However, we do know from the events of the last thirty or so years, the horrors of unlimited power. We are beginning, somewhat belatedly, to see the costs to individual freedom and richly diverse human personality that are inherent in the tendencies to mass society. This is one root of the present slackness in our politics. Few of us at present see any way out of a baffling dilemma. Bigness and concentration of power seem to be the prerequisite for material advance and for the extension of liberating opportunity, and at the same time the enemy of other humane values. The dilemma is just as serious for socialists as for other liberal democrats.

Hesitations caused by the dilemma have brought us, for the time being at least, to what has been called "the end of ideology," to the slipping of ardent convictions on what can be achieved through politics. Both moderate individualists and socialists used to have assurance in their diverse prescriptions for setting the conditions of the good life. Both are now unsure of some of their assumptions and values. There is some doubt about how broadly based is the desire for a vital individual freedom, as also about the compatibility of meaningful freedom with some of our other objectives. Ironically, it was easier to believe in the inherent dignity of the individual when we saw the gallantry of the struggle against heavy odds in poverty and privation than it is when we see the aimlessness of much of our consumption of leisure and other goods in the present day. When we watch the experts in applied psychology appeal to emotions and drive reason from the field, we sometimes wonder whether rational sequence is more than a freak form of mental activity. If rationality comes under suspicion, one of the props of the ardent faith in the people and in the coherence and sanity of the popular will begins to buckle. The people may not come to reasonable conclusions at all. In these circumstances, no confident political initiative springs from our tradition, and we are in the doldrums.

To get out of them, we need to decide whether the liberal faith in man, in its chastened and sceptical as distinct from its more optimistic form, is wrong, a gross misreading of his essential nature and of human possibilities. Or is it right with a vengeance? Is the proof now before us that human nature *is* malleable, that men *can* control their destiny, in regressive as well as progressive ways? Is it that in running our affairs over the last 200 years, we took a wrong turning and are creating forms of society that bias us to regress rather than progress? Is our trouble due to an earlier failure of intelligence to take full account of the problem rather than to any incurable defects of human nature?

In the end, we are unlikely to get utterly convincing answers to these questions, and we shall still have to go for a faith rather than a certainty. Having to conclude here without a certainty, I recall an important consideration bearing on a faith. The alternative to a generous faith in man is a craven faith in authority, freed, it is true, from responsibility to our fickle selves but still wielded by fallible men. In our present disenchantment with ourselves and our fellows, we should remember that long ago we were thoroughly disillusioned with authority, whether of priests, kings, or oligarchs.

Lightning Source UK Ltd.
Milton Keynes UK
UKHW012358200722
406167UK00001B/310